Success Secrets

from The

Three Little Pigs

10th Anniversary Edition

Robert Roots

New York, New York

Publishing & Distribution

www.RobertRoots.com

2nd Printing- September, 2012

ISBN: 978-0-9715336-3-9

Library of Congress Control Number: 2011962941

Printed in the United States of America

Dedication

I dedicate this book to my family and all who desire a better life.

To Get The Most From

Success Secrets from The Three Little Pigs

A) Read each section twice before moving on to the next section.

b) Highlight important ideas and write them down.

c) Review this book each month.

d) Have fun with the book. Determine if you have a Straw, Wood or Brick Mindset.

e) You reap what you sow. Give copies of this book to those who you know could benefit.

f) Make a list of your goals, devise a strategy and set deadlines.

g) Learn and Master the Seven C's of Success and the Bonus C.

h) Watch your words and conversations. Your mouth is the master key to your destiny!

I) Be The Brick! Live like it.

Contents

Success Secrets

from The

Three Little Pigs

Foreword

D o you remember the story about The Three Little Pigs? Even though it has been years since I heard the story, I can still feel the fear I experienced when I recall the part of the story when the big bad wolf was determined to huff, puff and blow the pigs house down and eat them up. It is amazing how a simple children's story can so engage you that it literally takes your mind to another place that you will never forget. Get ready for a deeper look at this classic children's tale.

Robert Roots masterfully transformed this age-old fairytale into a metaphor that shows you how to deal with the challenges of life that can cause us to fail. With creative genius and mind-expanding concepts from perhaps the age-old thinking, "An ounce of prevention is worth a pound of cure" Robert, with his unique approach warns with a loud voice of alarm, "The wolf is coming." So get ready, prepare and plan to defeat the wolf before he devours you.

No doubts our thoughts and actions reveal our strengths and weaknesses. Be our mindset- Straw, Wood or Brick- it will manifest conditions of solid character with dreams and purpose realized or as evidence of loosely structured values and beliefs that cause us to be co-conspirator in our own demise. Driven by fear and a lack of discipline, many people become volunteer victims in life by holding their talents and dreams hostage, refusing to participate in their own rescue.

Cornered and confronted by adverse circumstance called the "Big Bad Wolf" the situation for The Three Little Pigs appears to be hopeless. But wait, it ain't over yet. "Success Secrets from The Three Little Pigs" offers a unique and creative approach for overcoming obstacles and meeting the challenges that life brings our way. This book is loaded with insight, strategies and practical steps of faith required for living a life of purpose and meaning.

Those experiencing even the most difficult of circumstances can successfully apply these principles for overcoming trials and moving toward even greater triumphs. Robert Roots compels us to "Be the Brick"- people whom approach life with preparation, focus and discipline. Building our lives with the 7 C's of Success- Character, Commitment Confidence, Competence, Consistency, Creativity and Courage, Robert's convincing advice will lead you to achievement and fulfillment in life and business.

"Success Secrets from The Three Little Pigs" is not just another run of the mill book on motivation, it is a success guide skillfully designed to help you and the people you care about create a life of happiness and abundance. Scripture reminds us, "We must become as little children." With child like intrigue and adventure,

"Success Secrets from The Three Little Pigs" will put you on the path of living a life of value, excitement and contribution.

Les Brown

World Renowned Author and Motivational Speaker
Ranked in Top 5 Speakers in the World

The Three Little Pigs and Real Life

E ach year millions of people read The Three Little Pigs. It is read in schools and homes and there have been plays and cartoons depicting the story. Yet few people understand how The Three Little Pigs apply to life. Like many folk stories, its primary purpose has been for entertainment. However, with critical evaluation one discovers that The Three Little Pigs is truly a metaphor for life. It is about choices and how those choices affect our ability to prepare for the challenges in life.

The material each pig chose to build their home with represents their mindset, Straw, Wood and Brick. These are not just materials chosen by the three pigs, we as people also build our lives out of these very same materials. The homes the pigs live in represent life or the result of those choices. Whereas, the Wolf in the story is a metaphor for the obstacles and challenges we experience in life.

Most experts suggest if you want to succeed at a goal or task, you should envision what you want to accomplish or where you are going before you begin your journey. I agree, but there is another important factor to consider. If you want to reach a destination, not only is it important to know where you are going, it is equally important to know your starting point or your mindset.

Discovering which mindset you identify with most from the story of The Three Little Pigs— Straw, Wood or Brick— will help you understand where you are, the quality of choices you are making and will provide insight and foresight to where you may find yourself if you continue on the same path. This is an integral part of my copyrighted and trademarked Core Development Training for Organizations, Academia and Individuals - *Innerstanding*™ - which means an awareness and appreciation for one's purpose.

Just like in the story, there is a phrase in the sport of boxing regarding a person's chin. In boxing, your chin is an indication of your ability to take a punch. Metaphorically, your chin reflects your strength and ability to deal with life's challenges and obstacles. Each pig thought his chinny chin chin could stand up to the power of the Wolf. Just as the pigs discovered, it is not until facing a Wolf that you find out whether your choices will sustain you under the pressure of his huffing and puffing to blow your house in.

Most of the obstacles or Wolves you encounter, you invite into your life by the choices you make. When you learn to anticipate the consequences of everything you say, do, think, as well as the quality of your friends and associates, you limit the amount of Wolves you have to confront. Look at the pig who built his house of Wood. If he did not let the pig who built out of Straw in, then maybe the

Wolf would not have come in search of the Straw pig and blown his house down too.

Decide the strength and integrity of your life before you start to build. Build with a solid foundation and Brick building blocks so when the Wolf comes, he cannot huff and puff, and blow your house, hopes and dreams down. Unfortunately, many people do not prepare for the Wolf. They expect their lives to be perfect and problem free. No one's life is problem free. Obstacles and challenges confront each of us regardless of our backgrounds, race, gender, or size of our dreams. Everything you experience is a by-product of the choices that you or someone else has made. Life is a mathematical equation; today represents the sum total of all those choices.

The Wolf is cunning so be aware of your strengths and weaknesses.

Expect success, but be a realistic optimist. Accept the fact that obstacles and challenges are inevitable. Always have a contingency plan. Do not wait for the Wolf to be standing at your front door threatening to blow your house down before you prepare for him. By then it may be too late. Just like the Straw and Wood Pig, when the Wolf huffs, puffs and blows your house in, you will also wish you built your home out of Brick.

Maybe you have had a hard life, full of challenges and obstacles. Everybody has a story. It is you, who writes the end of your story. There are endless books on people who have triumphed against the odds. Read about them. The real odds are determined in your mind. If you think you cannot succeed, you will not. Believe in yourself, set goals, make a plan and take control of your life. Be conscious of the choices you make and the thoughts you allow into your mind. Program your mind for what you desire by meditating on those things only. Do not focus on the things you do not want.

Learn from challenges and disappointments, there is a reason they happen. These experiences are investments in your future. They will pay dividends later. Use the knowledge you gain to turn negatives into positives and to make better decisions. There are choices and consequences. You decide the consequences by the decisions you make. Life pays in exact measure. You reap what you sow. Be responsible with your decisions.

If you are waiting on others to take action for you, be prepared for a lifetime of disappointments and living someone else's dream, not yours. There is little satisfaction in life if you do not take responsibility for your life. In life as it is in war, the element of surprise is one of the most effective tools to winning. By planning and preparing, you deny the Wolf the opportunity to catch you by surprise.

Remember: *Your mindset determines the quality of your choices.*

Do You Have a Straw, Wood or Brick Mindset?

Y our life reflects your mindset. Some people believe they cannot choose to be successful and have to settle for mediocrity, while others just accept whatever life has to offer and see the daily struggle as permanent. However, each of us has the ability to be happy and successful. In fact, for most of us, the stage we are at in life, whether it is Straw, Wood or Brick, is a result of how we think and make choices. By changing your mindset, you will change your choices and ultimately your reality will change.

As you read about each of the three mindsets, determine which mindset you identify with most. Write this down in the notes section in the back of the book. Include reasons why you think you are Straw, Wood or Brick. Highlight the areas in your life you need to improve. Keep in mind that there are varying degrees for each mindset, but the basic attributes are the same.

Winning starts within. You control your thoughts and the quality of your life. The goal for your life should be to become Brick. Brick is a choice just like Straw and Wood. Straw and Wood people can become Brick. It is just a matter of changing your mindset and taking custody of your life. No condition in life is permanent. You decide its life span by the choices you make. Change your life by mastering your mindset.

As you assess your mindset, you will probably discover four things that you may need to implement to Be The Brick! For one, you may identify some things you need to stop doing such as procrastinating. Then there are some things you need to start doing, such as planning and writing down your goals. Next, there are things you may have to do less of such as spending money wastefully and wasting time on frivolous activities. Lastly, you may have to invest more of your time learning and enhancing your skills. All four of these activities, stopping, starting, doing less, and doing more, are all part of holding yourself accountable for your time, your focus, your outcomes and ultimately the success you experience.

Remember: *Reality begins in your mind and then manifests itself in your life.*

Straw Mindset

The Straw person does not plan his or her life. They leave everything to chance, living day-to-day, paycheck-to-paycheck. They do not expect much out of life. Some people believe they are not capable of being anything but Straw. They believe they are not good enough, nor smart enough to be Wood or Brick. Straw does not consider the consequences of their actions, their decisions, or the quality of people in their life. They make choices primarily from their emotions.

In school, Straw people are the non-achievers. Straw students are frequently absent without a legitimate reason. Their grades are usually failing and they do not seem to care about their future. They come unprepared for school. School is a social experience and not an educational one. Their mindset, not their intellectual capacity, is causing Straw people to fail or barely survive. Their Straw mindset is not allowing them to maximize their potential.

Straw students have the highest dropout rates and are frequently in altercations. Teachers describe these students to be the ones who are "just taking up space" because their grades, attendance, attitude and conduct indicate they are not in school to learn or to succeed in life.

Straw people are either unemployed or take the easiest job they can find. They tend to earn the least money and are usually the ones who complain about their salaries not being sufficient to live on. Instead of taking responsibility for their lives, find better employment or pursue higher education, they make excuses or blame others.

Straw spelled backwards is warts. Warts are a sign of problems or stress. It is like having leprosy. You can almost tell Straw people by looking in their face and

> *Straw has the ability to live their dreams; they just do not try.*

by their lifestyle. Just like a piece of Straw, they cannot stand up on their own. Straw feels the need to lean on something or someone for support. Straw gave up on life's possibilities.

Many people live like Straw. Straw is not limited to people of a particular age group, ethnicity or gender. Straw people surrender to the Wolf without a fight. When Straw people review their lives, they see few achievements and little happiness. They go through life without a vision and without a plan.

Remember: *If you fail to plan, plan to fail.*

Straw Story

Tony and I were classmates in elementary school. Just like other kids, he had dreams of being rich famous and chauffeured in a stretch limousine. Academically he was an average student but played sports better than most people our age. At the age of eleven, he was already playing basketball and baseball after school with the guys from high school. By the time we started middle school, he was famous in the neighborhood for his athletic ability. Most people expected him to at least play college sports even if not in the major leagues or NBA.

Many years later while I was a police officer working on Times Square in New York City, I heard someone call my name. When I turned around there was Tony. Surprised, I gave Tony a hug and told him how happy I was to see him. On the corner a few feet from where we were standing was a fast food restaurant so we went there to talk and have breakfast.

Tony informed me that he quit high school in the tenth grade. The school work was too hard. Then he started working low paying jobs and fixing cars while he hustled on the street. Looking at

Tony, I saw regret in his eyes. Staring at the ground, he said, "In my next life, I'll make it."

Oddly enough, I had recently bought a used car that was having mechanical trouble. After sharing my problems with Tony, he suggested I meet him with the car that afternoon in front of the restaurant. When I arrived, he revealed he did not have many tools but he believed he could fix the car anyway. Two hours later the car was running like new. After paying Tony, I gave him my phone number to stay in touch. I figured I could refer him some business and we could reminisce about our childhood. Tony never called.

A few months later, while visiting friends in the old neighborhood, I saw Tony again. I told him that the owner of the car dealership said that mechanics like him are hard to come by. The owner said few people could have fixed my car without a computer and especially in only a couple of hours. Knowing that Tony needed employment, I gave him the car dealer's phone number and told him I would drive him to the dealership. No call once again.

While writing this book, I happened to see Tony's mother. She said that she did not understand what happened to Tony. She said Tony lost focus in school, had failing grades and instead of studying, he gave up. Foolishly, Tony thought he could quit high school and a professional sports scout would pick him up while playing street ball. That did not happen. When Tony's mother suggested he reenroll in school, he refused. He said the process was too long and he did not like classrooms.

Tony's mother was very hurt to see her son lose out in life and not use his talents to his full potential. His mother and I have both witnessed his incredible ability to master whatever he chose to do. The only one who did not see his potential and opportunities was Tony. There are people like Tony everywhere. Some stand on street corners day after day. They have no plans. They feel hopeless and helpless. Some work for low wages, earning barely enough to survive and are usually victims of their own choices regarding education, friends and lifestyle. Past choices put them where they are, but their mindset keeps them there. You always have a choice. Do not be a Tony and do not be Straw.

Remember: *There is no next life. It is now or never.*

Wood Mindset

T he Wood person settles for mediocrity. Wood is straddling the fence between knowing how to live their dreams and wanting things to come easy or a simply failing to take action to make things happen. Most of the time Wood people are not satisfied with the success they do have because they know they are capable of achieving more but settled for less.

In school, Wood people are under-achievers. Wood settles for a lower grade than they are capable of achieving. Their schoolwork usually does not reflect their abilities. They just want to achieve good grades, not the best of their capabilities. Teachers describe Wood students as not living up to their potential. They are not disruptive or excessively absent from school. Wood people tend to be struggling with the Wolves of doubt, fear, procrastination and excuses.

On teams or at work, Wood people do just enough to stay on the team or employed. They say things like, "It's not my job" or "I would, but." Wood see others being promoted and achieving extraordinary success and want the same for themselves but are hampered by their Straw/ weak side.

Most people are Wood. They see the benefits that a little more effort will bring and are capable of reaching their goals or dreams but fall short. Wood people understand the consequences of their choices but make excuses for themselves. In fact, Wood tries to show the world their Brick side while hiding their Straw side. Doing this places limitations in their lives. They avoid taking leadership positions or getting too involved in activities for fear others will discover their weakness.

Wood spelled backwards is two words, Do and Ow. Wood knows what to do to live his or her dreams but wants to avoid the discomfort of sacrifice to reach their goals. Instead, Wood people feel the pain later in life knowing they settled for

> *A chain is as strong as its weakest link. For Wood their weak link is their Straw side.*

less. They know if they had sacrificed and did not settle they would have achieved their goals.

Wood people give in. They have dreams, plans and abilities but detour from the path. They typically earn average incomes; their things to do lists are rarely complete and they tend to have a lot of unfinished business. Wood people have the most regrets in life because there is nothing worse than knowing you could have achieved more but did not and the main reason is you.

Remember: *The real pain in life is a failure to take action.*

Wood Story

I t was a high school graduation and I was the keynote speaker. As I mingled among the students prior to the ceremony, I heard graduates talking about their experiences, hopes and dreams. One student sat in the auditorium with tears in her eyes. Her name was Victoria. I sat with her and asked what was wrong. She said that her college of choice did not accept her. Instead, she would be attending her last choice.

Victoria knew what college she wanted to attend. She even took a trip to the school while in the eighth grade with her parents to look at the campus and meet with the admissions counselor. She knew the school's admission criteria. What troubled her was that if she had applied herself, her first choice would have accepted her.

Victoria always set goals and was very ambitious. She was involved in martial arts and music. When she started studying karate at the age of ten, her goal was to become a black belt. She studied until the age of fifteen, when she quit as a brown belt, just one belt from black belt. Her reason for quitting, she formed a band and wanted to record a single in attempt to get a record deal. Victoria even convinced a recording studio to write songs and provide free recording for her group. She told them she would give them referral business in addition to a percentage of money earned if the song came out. Then one day she stopped showing up to recording sessions citing other responsibilities.

When it came to school, Victoria did not consider certain classes important so she did just enough to make sure she got a passing grade. She did not realize these classes and her conduct would affect her grade point average and reputation. She thought her first choice would accept her because she excelled in everything else and she could convince the school to overlook the rules.

Victoria was capable of attaining her black belt but did not because she quit too soon. She negotiated a recording deal but does not have a finished record to show for it. The other members of the group finished the record without her. When it came to school, she knew the college criteria but still slacked off. Victoria was not committed to achieving her goals or else she would have achieved them.

Victoria is like most people. They know how to accomplish what they want and are fully capable of doing so. They can even have the path to success in writing but still fall short. Even when they have some success, they do not enjoy it because they are constantly trying to hide their shortcomings and are aware of the fact that they could have achieved more.

Remember: *It is not enough to know what you do; you still have to do.*

Brick Mindset

B rick people plan their lives. Brick understands there is no substitute for success. They are fully aware of the Wolf; in fact, they have encountered him before. Brick people are aware that the people you invite into your life can bring the Wolf with them. Brick people choose their friends and associates carefully.

In school, Brick people are the achievers. They are the students who plan their study time and do their best. Being Brick does not mean you get the highest grade in class, it just means you do your best. It is possible to be an average student and still be Brick.

Brick people are at all levels of society and the work environment. Regardless of their position at the company or on the team, they bring value to the organization. Brick people find ways to give more than what they are paid. They take pride in what they do because they know their work reflects who they are. Brick people are willing to educate themselves, seek out new and creative ways to achieve their goals and understand the value of teamwork. They manage their time and money while focusing on needs not wants.

Brick people do not reflect over their lives with regrets or disappointments. They use life experiences as lessons and stepping-stones. Brick people know that if you do not learn from the past, history will repeat itself.

Brick people never give in to the Wolf. They are the happiest and most successful of the three mindsets. Brick people finish what they start and are usually the highest wage earners. Both their personal and professional lives are balanced and successful.

Brick people have conversations about success and achieving extraordinary dreams. They look forward to the morning and

> *Brick people follow through and finish what they start.*

accomplishing their goals. It is no wonder that Straw and Wood run to Brick people when they have problems and are running from the Wolf.

Remember: *Brick people plan, prepare and pursue their goals.*

Brick Story

Carlos Santiago was born in South America and was raised there until the age of thirteen when his family relocated to the United States in search of a better life. Though Carlos did not speak English, he did not want to waste time waiting for the school system to teach him. Being raised in another country and experiencing an unstable government and extreme poverty, Carlos was not going to let anything stop him from achieving his goals.

After school, Carlos volunteered in the school library shelving books. He used that time to learn English by reading book titles and by completing basic paperwork. He borrowed English-speaking cassette tapes from the library and listened to them in his headphones on the way to and from school. One of the cassettes he listened to was on financial planning. Though he did not fully understand all the terminology, he did not let that stop him. Instead, he began keeping a journal and used a dictionary. Then he started listening to tutorial tapes on starting a business and on different careers. With these, he also kept a journal.

When it came time to attend college, he was already bilingual. Having mastered the internet, he located college scholarships and various grants, which he applied for and received. With the money he earned working weekends at the grocery store, he started a savings account. With part of his money, he started a business. The business closed a year later. Then he started three more and they too closed. Finally, after four attempts he found one that worked. Using his life experiences he started a tutoring service for Spanish speaking students where he taught English, basic business courses and money management.

I met Carlos in Miami, Florida, while he and I were there receiving business achievement awards. In fact, Carlos was receiving multiple awards. As they read his biography, I looked around expecting to see him walk up to the front. He did not. He rolled up to the front of the room in a wheelchair. Carlos lost his legs at the age of four due to his family not having money for medical care.

Carlos is not disabled; only his legs are. Disability begins in the mind. Carlos had a dream and was not willing to fail. He made a promise to himself that he would never let anything or his condition stop him from success. If he started something, he would finish it. Having experienced tragedy and poverty, he learned from them. He did not expect things to come easy but he knew if someone else succeeded and others wrote about it then it is possible. You can overcome any obstacle. Every person has challenges. Manage your life so that your mindset does not become your greatest handicap or obstacle.

Remember: *Anyone can start; it takes a winner to finish.*

Are You Afraid Of The Big Bad Wolf?

A s I mentioned earlier, the Wolf confronts all of us. Whether you are Straw, Wood or Brick, you will face challenges and obstacles in life. The Wolf can be defeated. First, you must plan and prepare before the Wolf is knocking at your door.

When the Wolf could not blow down the Brick pig's house, he entered through the chimney. The chimney is a metaphor for your brain or your thoughts. Preparing for the Wolf, the Brick pig placed a pot of water over a fire inside the chimney destroying the Wolf. If the Brick pig had let him dwell inside his home, the Wolf would have destroyed him from inside.

Do not internalize a problem. If you do, it will cause stress and it will prevent you from achieving your goals. "As a man thinketh, so is he". When you control a person's mind, you control the person. By allowing a problem to consume you, it preoccupies your thoughts, actions and attitude.

Preparation is the first step to victory.

Address problems immediately and effectively by planning and implementing. As you go through challenges, grow through them. Some of life's greatest lessons occur during times of trials and tribulations. The way you handle obstacles and challenges affects every area of your life, your future, your career, your happiness and your success.

According to M. Scott Peck, author of the best-seller, The Road Less Traveled, "...it is in this whole process of meeting and solving problems that life has its meaning. Problems are the cutting edge that distinguishes between success and failure. Problems call forth our courage and our wisdom; indeed, they create our courage and our wisdom. It is only because of problems that we grow mentally and spiritually... It is through the pain of confronting problems that we learn."

Following are ten of the most common Wolves we experience in life. There are other Wolves. If you fail to prepare for these Wolves, you will bring more to your doorstep.

(Life is a mirror image of our choices. Flow spelled backwards is Wolf. When your life does not flow and you are stuck or challenged, you are more than likely facing a Wolf.)

Fear

F ear is probably the most common Wolf we encounter. A variety of factors can cause fear, some of them are real but most of them created in your mind. Most of us fear that we will not succeed at a given goal or task. The fear of not succeeding has two major side effects. One side effect is that you can become almost paralyzed or withdraw emotionally. The other is that you avoid starting or quit before finishing. Sometimes, the fear is that you might succeed and the responsibilities that come with success.

The key to overcoming fear is to keep in mind that ninety-five percent of the things you fear do not actually happen. Separate feelings of fear from reality. Do things that reinforce your confidence. Recall a time when you were afraid of pursuing a goal but you tried and succeeded. In the case of a new job or career, remind yourself that you are capable of doing the job and that is the reason you have the opportunity. Opportunity comes to those who are able. You decide if you are ready and willing.

In any new experience, there is a learning curve and you should leave room for mistakes. Repeat to yourself, "I can, I will, I am, if someone else has done it, it can be done." "I earned and deserve this opportunity!" No matter what happens, you will have learned something new. Everybody has fears. The person who gives in to fear becomes a victim to it. If fear wins, you lose. Use fear to motivate you.

Remember: *You can either live your life or live your fears!*

"Your ears create fears"

S top listening to other people. They do not determine your future. Many times other people contribute to our fears by focusing on the negative. Fear is an emotion that you can use to motivate or deter you.

Since I was six years old, my dream was to become a New York City Police Officer. I was excited when at the age of sixteen I became eligible to take the police exam. Prior to the test, some friends and family talked to me about the dangers of police work and described the Police Academy as a military boot camp. At first, I ignored their comments but the more I heard the more convinced I became that the job was not for me. As a result, I almost changed my mind.

After encouragement from my mother, I decided to take the police exam in spite of the fears everyone else was projecting on me. When I received my test score, to my surprise, I achieved a 98.3, placing me in the top 1% of the 15,000 test takers.

On January 20, 1987, at the age of twenty, I started the New York City Police Academy. Without a doubt, attending the Police Academy and the experience I gained as a Police Officer has helped me to develop into the person I am today. Even though I left police work years later to pursue entrepreneurial opportunities, I submit to you, even more than my decision to become an author, entrepreneur, consultant and professional speaker, becoming a police officer was the single best career decision I have ever made. Had I listened to other people and gave in to the fear; I may not have lived my childhood dream nor have the knowledge of the incredible police training I received.

Remember: *You do not have to be fearless. Just fear less.*

Procrastination

Procrastination is putting off things for later when you should be doing them now. Procrastination is even more detrimental to success than fear. Most of us know when we are afraid; it consumes us, sometimes speaking to us subconsciously. Procrastination is the silent killer. Most people procrastinate and do not realize it.

A multitude of factors may cause procrastination. One is perfectionism. Instead of starting or completing a project, the perfectionist is always working on it. If you are waiting for perfection, you will never be finished because nothing will ever be perfect. Stop looking for perfection. Do the best you can and move on, there are more goals you need to achieve.

Maybe you are waiting for the right time. There are times better than other times but studies show the longer you wait, the less likely you will do something. If you are planning to open a business, taking a new position, furthering your education or making any other major life changes, consider the cost of waiting and not doing it right now.

Some procrastinators purposely do not prioritize their time and resources to avoid being uncomfortable. Think of the pleasure you will gain from reaching your goals and the regret you will experience if you do not reach them. Start now. Organize your time and resources by order of importance and challenge yourself to complete your goals. Set deadlines. Deadlines will keep you on schedule and serve as a gauge of how focused and committed you are.

There are no rewards until you finish, get started today!

Ask someone you respect to keep you on task. Send them a list of your goals and time-lines. Have them e-mail or call to remind you of the pending deadlines. Place the list on your computer, refrigerator or mirror as a daily reminder. Reward yourself for completing on time by buying yourself something special. Penalize yourself for not completing on time by not buying something you want until you are finished.

Remember: *Do not delay; get started today.*

"Maximum effort, yields minimum risk!"

I f you want to reduce your risk, put more time and energy into reaching your goals. You become more familiar with the pitfalls and the solutions. A primary reason for people failing to reach their goals is that they procrastinate and do not commit enough time to their goals. Experts become experts by investing time and becoming competent at what they do.

You get out of life, what you put in and you cannot wait until tomorrow to do it. When in school, study as much as you can for as long as you can. At work, care enough to do your best. The difference between those who achieve and those who do not is usually due to how much quality time and effort they give to their goals and responsibilities.

I have learned that the people who make the most money in business do research about the business in which they are investing, understand the marketplace, look at the future business climate and maximize their creativity, thus limiting their risk factor. After gathering information, successful people make decisions quickly and without hesitation.

There will always be risk in pursuing any goal. The key is to limit the risk by gathering enough information to make intelligent decisions and avoid procrastinating. Consider this, if you do not take the risk, you are already telling yourself no. You are defeated before getting started. Get started and you will be rewarded with the experience and the pride of doing and pursuing. You are able but you will never know if you do not do it.

Remember: *Successful people make up their minds quickly and change them slowly.*

Excuses

S ome people disguise excuses as explanations. Excuses do not pay bills, bring joy nor offer opportunity. We all fall short of completing our goals and some of our responsibilities from time to time, but do not take comfort in excuses. Excuses tend to blame factors such as your age, ethnicity, time; resources, distractions, obligations and even your abilities but these are not real barriers. Committed people find a way in spite of the real and perceived obstacles.

If you are continuously making excuses, you need to decide how important your dreams are. To determine if they are important and critical to making you more successful, write them down on a piece of paper. Draw a line down the page and write on one side "wins" and on the other side "losses." Write down what you will gain by accomplishing your goals and what you will lose if you do not. Keep in mind that your "wins" and "losses" extend beyond this particular goal.

As mentioned earlier, your life is the sum total of your decisions. Make a decision to eliminate all excuses. Excuses negatively affect your future and become habit forming. Once you find it easy to make excuses, you will make excuses for your excuses. Develop the courage and character to make things happen. The more excuses you make, the less successful and happy you will be. In fact, you are teaching others to do the same. Do not settle for excuses, the people counting on you will not either.

Remember: *Excuses are a curse to your goals.*

"It's not what you don't have; it's what you think you need that stops you from succeeding or being happy!"

M ost people do not start a business, pursue their goals or apply for a new job or position because they think they do not have enough money, education, experience or contacts. If you appreciate what you do have and maximize your resources, then you will discover that you already possess what you need to get started and in many cases succeed. Most people you meet in life are not aware of what you have or do not have. You reveal this information to them.

An example of this is when my friend April applied for a job in the marketing department at a large entertainment company. She submitted her application and received an interview. Though April was nervous and did not have a lot of experience in the industry, she did not want her fears to be an excuse for her not pursuing her goals. During the interview, she told the recruiter why she wanted to work with the company and the value that she could bring to the organization.

After her interview, some of our friends pointed out to April that she did not have any contacts or experience in the entertainment industry. When I saw the hesitation and doubt in April's eyes because of what our friends were saying, I stepped in. I explained to them instead of focusing on what April lacked, we needed to focus on what she has; extensive life experiences, a degree in a related field, a strong ability to do research and an incredible amount of success in other areas of her life.

When April was hired, all of our friends now had a story about a time when the odds seemed stacked against them. They too remembered that when they focused on their strengths and not their weaknesses, they achieved their goals too.

This had been one of my greatest challenges. I focused on what I did not have. I thought I was not qualified to pursue some of my life's goals. I saw people with less education, experience, and resources succeed in areas I did not think I could have succeeded. I talked myself out of my goals. It was not until I changed my mindset and stopped making excuses did things change for me.

We tend to overestimate what it takes to win and underestimate our abilities and resources. In fact, once you get started, everything you need seems to fall into place. First, you have to stop finding excuses not to do and find reasons why you can and should do what you desire.

Remember: *You paint the picture people see!*

Doubt

D oubt or uncertainty happens when you are unsure of your abilities. A lack of confidence due to your past, limited education, other people's opinions or lack of experience can cause doubt. If you think you are not capable of succeeding then you will think like a failure. Your thinking affects your actions. When you act like a failure, you will become a failure because you stop trying and stop looking for solutions.

Winning starts within. Within you lies the power to accomplish almost anything you set your mind to. If a lack of education is the cause, seek it out. Learning is a never-ending process. Do not let education stop you. If you think education is expensive, try ignorance.

Some doubters think they need to wait on others for support or approval. Waiting on others denies you the opportunity to learn and to take pride in

If it is to be, success is up to me.

accomplishing your goals. Furthermore, you probably will never begin. If you absolutely do not know what to do, then seek assistance. There is nothing wrong with asking for help. It takes courage to be humble. As Les Brown says, "Ask for help not because you are weak; ask for help because you want to remain strong."

Push past the doubt. Keep working towards your goals. With each step, you will develop more skill and confidence. Focus on finishing your immediate and short-range goals first. As you see yourself making progress, you will become more effective, more powerful and more determined to succeed.

Remember: *Doubt is another way of telling yourself, NO!*

"Falling isn't failing; it's part of the process!"

We all fall when we learn something new, just like when we first learned how to ride a bicycle. If you do not have the courage to try again, you will begin to doubt yourself and may never learn. When I started my consulting and speaking careers, I experienced highs and lows or, as they say in business, peaks and valleys. Every time I found myself in the valley, I learned something new. I learned what went wrong, and how to avoid falling and making the same mistakes.

I remember my first business venture while in high school; I quit the first time I had some obstacles. I felt like a failure. Then I discovered that even though the business failed that I was not a failure. If it were not for the hard times and trying in spite of the struggles, I probably would not appreciate the good times as much as I do. A fall teaches you a lesson. You learn how to find solutions to problems. When you see yourself as a failure, you give up and stop trying because you lose confidence and begin to doubt yourself. I learned that I can fall but I can get back up and win.

Most great achievements and long-term relationships have experienced challenges. There probably would not be any fifty year wedding anniversaries, technological advances or successful people if they were not committed enough to endure in spite of the challenges. Do not be afraid to fall. Everyone falls. With it, come some of life's greatest lessons and opportunities. Use a fall to motivate you to do things differently and better. This is how you learn and come to appreciate your blessings. A fall becomes a failure when you look at yourself and the experience negatively. Falling is not failing; it is part of the success process.

Remember: *Do not ask why me. Instead ask, what can I learn from this experience?*

Criticism

C riticism is one of the main causes for depression and low
self-esteem. Criticism can cause pain, fear and
procrastination. It can also reduce your confidence level and have
countless other character destroying affects. Separate criticism from
good advice. Even when meant to be helpful, criticism can be
harmful and destructive to your self-esteem. Some people who
criticize do so to cover up their own shortcomings or inadequacies.
Do not let other people's problems become yours. Always consider
the source and the motive.

When pursuing a goal, regard other people's advice in the
proper context. They are expressing their own opinion which does
not necessarily make them correct. It is okay and quite healthy to
believe that you may have the solution or the right answers. Use
other people's advice to make an honest evaluation to see if there
are things that need improvement. When you identify areas to work
on, make adjustments, but do not criticize yourself.

Be aware that not all criticism comes from other people. Some
people are much more critical of themselves than other people
could ever be. This is self-destructive. Correct your actions but do

not destroy who you are. For everything that needs correction, there are probably a thousand more things right about you and your ideas. Do not be afraid to make mistakes and do not let mistakes become deterrents. It is best to test your ideas and give them a chance. You never know what lies ahead. Besides, who made the critics the authority on what is possibly for your ideas and your life. Give yourself permission to win and go for it. You deserve to win.

Remember: *Love Yourself.*

"Don't take a poll, take control!"

S top surveying your friends, family and sometimes strangers before you make a decision. If you have an idea, take the time, do research and decide what you are going to do. There is always more than one way to accomplish a goal. When you survey people by asking for their opinions and suggestions, you leave yourself vulnerable to possible criticism.

This reminds me of my friend and the person who wrote the foreword for this book, author and motivational speaker Les Brown. He often shares a story with his audiences about the time he told his friends that one day he would be known as "The Motivator." Laughing at him, they told him to get a job in Sanitation and to forget the Post Office because there you had to take a test. Few people supported Les and most criticized his dream.

> *Do not let criticism stop you from achieving your dreams.*

More than 20 years ago, I first met Les Brown via a telephone call through a mutual friend. The reason for the call was that I ordered his first cassette tapes and wanted to thank him for him being a great motivator. As you see, Les Brown did it in spite of other people's criticisms. Moreover, his products were the first motivational tapes I ever owned. His story and message inspired me to do what I do today. If Les Brown had let criticism stop him, maybe I would not be an entrepreneur, speaker, consultant, author or living my dreams.

What are you allowing criticism to stop you from achieving or being? You are reading this book for a reason. Do not let this moment pass you by. Encourage yourself.

Remember: *Rise above criticism and you rise above failure.*

Debt

U se sound judgment when it comes to your finances. Distinguish between wants and needs. You need clothing, food, shelter and basic transportation. Jewelry, expensive cars and overpriced name-brand goods are wants, not needs. Contrary to popular belief, material possessions and false images are nothing. The most valuable commodity in life you cannot own. Nothing can take the place of having people in your life that you love and respect, and that love and respect you.

In business, many people think they need to look the part to get the part. Many times this is true. Most times though you can creatively look the part without spending a lot of money. Shop at garage sales and at thrift shops. Adopt the attitude that less is more. Be responsible with your money. Debt is a major cause of stress and can distract you from your goals. Debt, just like problems are always easy to get in to but hard to get out.

The following are some basic tips to managing your money and creating wealth. These tips do not replace sound financial advice. These are only a guide to get you started in managing your money and financial habits:

- Develop a budget and stick to it.
- Save at least 15 % of your income.
- Avoid using credit cards and applying for too many credit cards.
- Pay off all non tax deductible debt as soon as possible.
- Save 6 months of expenses in an emergency account.
- Buy used items instead of a new when possible and economical.
- Take advantage of available tax deductions.
- Invest in appreciable assets.
- Create multiple streams of income.
- Start a business.

Remember: *Any fool can go into debt; it takes a wise person to avoid it.*

"Don't deal with the branches, deal with the roots"

After college, a classmate of mine found himself in an incredible amount of debt. Credit card bills were past due and creditors were calling. His car payments were late and he was struggling financially. When we met to discuss his situation, I asked him for a list of all of his outstanding debts. Instead of just coming up with a solution for paying off his debts, I examined his spending habits. Writing a check and paying off the debts would not have solved the problem. The debts were by-products of his not being committed to a budget.

A few years earlier, he had a similar amount of debt and his solution was to pay off the debt without examining the cause. Because he dealt with the branches, the debts, and not the root of his debt problems, which was his lack of discipline, the debts reoccurred. Now when he has a problem, be it financial or otherwise, he has learned to dig deeper to discover the real cause of the problem and then make the necessary adjustments.

Whenever you are facing a major challenge, look at how the problem began. When you make better decisions, you reduce the amount of challenges you face. You are responsible for most of the things you experience in life whether it is pleasant or unpleasant.

Take responsibility for your life. Do not think you cannot change your circumstances, you can. Sometimes the solution is making some minor adjustments and other times it will require you to make some major decisions. Whatever the solution turns out to be, nothing will change until you implement the changes.

You must look deeper than the situation. Most things do not just happen overnight. You may have to go as far back as your childhood to discuss the root causes. When you do, you will also discover how this issue has affected other parts of your life setting off a chain reaction and with it, consequences. If you resolve just the immediate crisis and not the cause, you will experience it again in some form or another.

Remember: *When resolving a problem, you have to get to the root or origin of the problem.*

Competition

D o not let competition stop you from pursuing your goals. Do not take your employer, clients or family for granted. Someone always wants what you have. Never think that you are indispensable. No one is indispensable. The service you give determines your worth to a company. Even if paid by the hour, your pay is not about time. Your pay is for the quality of service you give.

Competition means your dreams are worth pursuing and that others also see the value. Use competition to motivate you to be the best you can be. Competition is what makes champions reach beyond their grasp and accomplish feats previously unheard of. Competition is a major catalyst for change and progress. Without competition, inferior products and incompetence would be the standard. Learn from your competition. Find out what skills or abilities they possess and emulate them.

Give more than what people expect of you and more than what people are accustomed to receiving. Build strong relationships. Relationships give you the edge and lead to lasting friendships. Respect the people in your life and they will respect and be loyal to you. Competition means you have to continue to educate yourself and appreciate your blessings or someone else will. At the end of the day, you should be competing with yourself to be your best and give your best. When you do, you discover there is enough room for everyone, even your competition, to experience all that life has to offer.

Remember: *Compete with yourself to always do better next time.*

"Don't focus on success, focus on the steps and success will follow"

Success is a process. You earn a degree only after taking each of the required classes one at a time and passing the necessary examinations one question at a time. If you focus on competing with your classmates and try to take too many classes in one semester then you probably will not succeed.

When I was in college, some of us were more concerned with having the degree than mastering the skills. We wanted the degree instantly. We did not respect the process and quit before graduating. There is a saying, "You can pay me now or pay me later." This saying is especially true when it comes to education. Take the time to learn the skills necessary to achieve your objective and do not concern yourself with the outcome. The diploma or the degree will come when your part is complete not before.

The same is true for starting a business. If you overly concern yourself with becoming a multi-million dollar company rather than focusing on your company's structure and growing one customer at a time, you will lose your business before you get started. A company grows one customer at a time just as you graduate from school by completing one class at a time.

The key to achieving any goal is to identify what is necessary, the order things need to happen, and to do first things first. The key to building a house is to first lay a solid foundation and then build it one brick at a time. There is less stress and more success when you focus on the steps rather than the competition or the finished product. Be patient and committed. Do not set unrealistic goals or unrealistic deadlines or you will probably give up out of frustration.

Success is like walking; just put one foot in front of the other.

Remember: *Inch by inch, it is a cinch.*

Temptation

Y ou only have twenty-four hours in a day. If you subtract eight hours for sleeping, four hours for eating and other necessities, two hours for travel and eight hours for work or school, you only have two hours per day for yourself. How you use those hours is critical. Use your time effectively by organizing your day and prioritizing your responsibilities.

Temptation can cause you to sacrifice needs to obtain wants. Do not be tempted by outward appearances. Develop discipline and self-control. Do not give into lusts and wants. Learn to tell yourself no. Temptation can distract you from your goals and dreams. A feeling of guilt usually accompanies giving in to temptation. The guilt is your conscience chastising you for failing to exercise self-discipline. Lack of self-discipline will lead you down the wrong path. Weigh the cost of temptation. If it is not part of your larger plan, leave it alone.

Be true to yourself. Accepting the truth shall set you free from unnecessary distractions. Do not sacrifice your future for temporary satisfaction. The greatest enjoyment is experienced when you appreciate the discipline and dedication it took to accomplish your goals and objectives. Shortcuts and distractions invariably lead to disappointment. You are closer to achieving your goals than you realize. Do not allow temptation to stop you or delay your success.

Remember: *A straight line is always faster than a crooked one.*

"Success comes from sacrifice, sacrifice from self-discipline, and self-discipline from self-awareness."

W hen you are aware of who you are and what you want out of life, you see the benefits of self-discipline. The more disciplined you are, the easier it is to resist temptation and sacrifice your time and resources to reach your goals. Self-awareness is accepting the truth about yourself, your strengths, and your weaknesses. It is impossible to exercise self-discipline if you do not know yourself.

It is true that some do achieve success without self-awareness. They seem to have everything but are unhappy. They experience bouts of depression and are tempted to heal their suffering through drug and/or alcohol abuse. After obtaining material possessions, fame or prestige, they struggle with trying to discover who they really are and what they really want out of life. Unfortunately, neither money nor fame can buy happiness.

You experience true peace and happiness when you know your authentic self. Take the time to meditate and pray. Through this process of developing innerstanding™ you will discover the most important factor in your quest for success and happiness-YOU!

Remember: *Know Thyself.*

Past

Your past is not your future. Do not judge yourself based on past choices or experiences. We all make mistakes and will continue to make mistakes. The key is to learn and grow from those experiences. Do not let your past cripple you. Forgive yourself. The same is true for past success. Do not become complacent or arrogant. Always remain humble. Life does not make any guarantees, nor does it play favorites. It is never too late to succeed and it is never too late to turn success into failure.

Use past experiences as stepping-stones. Learn yesterday's lessons but leave yesterday in the past. Avoid self-pity. Self-pity is a very powerful and destructive force. It leads to discouragement, and defeat. Move on. Today is a new day and with it come new challenges and opportunities that need your undivided attention. Just like the past, you decide your future by the choice you make today.

Remember: *You cannot move forward looking backwards, if you do, you may stumble and fall.*

"If you do not have the power to change yourself, nothing will change around you."

M ost of the things you experience in life are a result of the choices you have made. To change what you are experiencing or going through, you need to change your choices. The events in your life as well as the people in your life, reflect the decisions you are making. Until you change your mindset, your reflection will not change. It is about personal accountability.

You cannot wait on conditions to improve first. You must take control of your life by mastering your mindset. Other people can give you advice but you determine the quality of your life. Your decisions divide your life in two— before the decision and after. Make sure that after is better than before. Not to make a decision is making a decision.

Many people complain about their condition in life but refuse to take action. They tell everyone the same story day after day hoping someone else fixes their problems. These people are the least satisfied with their lives. Things will not change for them or you, until you accept that you alone are responsible for your life, not anyone else.

Remember: *Everything starts and ends with you!*

Support

Not everyone will believe in your dreams. This includes friends and family. One of the challenges to pursuing your dreams is trying to convince others to agree with you or understand your dreams. Unless you need their support, it is best not to share your plans with too many people. Most people cannot see beyond their own circumstances or goals. Do not expect them to understand yours.

For some of you, a lack of family support could lead to family problems or a deferment of your dreams. Evaluate your goals and find a way to identify any areas that might be causing the disagreement. Make sure your dream is not selfish, unrealistic, or harmful to others. Share your goals with your family detailing objectives, timelines, *Support usually comes after you start, not before.* expectations and benefits. Be sure to express your desire for their love, support and encouragement. Your family is no different from other people, they too sometimes cannot see beyond their own circumstances or dreams. Make sure you maintain communication. Communication is the key to effective relationships.

Surround yourself with people who will support, encourage and guide you. To have a friend, you must first be a friend. Be a friend by supporting others who are also working on achieving their dreams. This support will return support for your aspirations. With or without other people's endorsement, you have to decide what you want and make it happen. As long as you believe and implement your ideas, your dreams stand a chance of becoming a reality. If not, then you will not achieve your dreams.

Remember: *The critical support you need comes from you, no one else!*

"When you are ready, a mentor appears!"

When you are ready, a mentor appears. If you want something bad enough, you send energy out into the world that you are looking for a mentor and one finds you. After you experience this phenomenon of help arriving when you need it, you develop the courage to work on your goals even when it seems the odds are not in your favor. Contrary to what is believed, most people like helping others to become successful.

Keep this in mind- You do not have to be great to get started but you have to get started to become great. Do not try to accomplish everything at once. Look at what you want to achieve and divide it into pieces. Complete what is necessary. Do the most important things first. Once you start, you will think differently and will naturally begin to creatively search for solutions and opportunities. During these times, you attract the resources you need. Mentors find you when they see you are taking responsibility for your goals.

Remember: *Do not worry about needing help, help will find you.*

The 7 C's of Success

In this section, we will discuss the qualities Brick people possess and implement in their lives. I refer to them as the 7 C's of Success: Character, Commitment, Confidence, Competence, Consistency, Creativity and Courage.

As I mentioned earlier, being Straw, Wood or Brick is a choice. Anyone can learn and apply the 7 C's of Success to make major changes in their lives. There is a saying, "Insanity is doing the same things repeatedly expecting different results." For some, the quote sounds familiar, for others, you have just discovered that you have been acting insane.

None of you would buy seeds that could not grow. So why would you settle for a life that is stuck or stagnant? With change comes growth. Growth cannot happen without change. If you want to change your life, change your mindset. Your mindset affects your attitude and your attitude determines your choices.

Just like at the end of The Three Little Pigs, after Straw and Wood saw the benefits of preparing for the Wolf, they too built homes made of Brick. Mastering the Seven C's will lead you to

Brick, allow you to defeat the Wolf and achieve happiness and success.

Remember: *Choose to Master the Seven C's and Be The Brick!*

Character

"The ultimate measure of a man is not where he stands in moments of comfort, but where he stands in time of challenge and controversy."
Rev. Dr. Martin Luther King, Jr.

The most important quality a person can possess is character. Character comes from a person's spirit and soul. It is the reservoir from which all your decisions flow. If you lack character, you will find yourself making decisions that will lead you down a Straw path. Character is about integrity, honesty and morality. A developed character possesses self-control, respects and achieves respect from others.

Commitment

"The quality of a person's life is in direct proportion to their commitment to excellence, regardless of their chosen field of endeavor."
Vince Lombardi

Commitment is the giving of you to your word and aspirations. Commitment helps you to develop endurance. When you are committed, you do not waiver in your decisions. Achieving your goal is your priority. Because you have totally given of yourself, you want and expect the best possible outcome. A lack of commitment creates chaos, hesitancy and doubt. When others see you are committed, they work to help you make it happen.

Confidence

"Clear your mind of can't."
Samuel Johnson

Confidence is belief in you, your abilities and possibilities. Confidence begets enthusiasm. Confidence says, "Try and try again." Confidence knows no limitations and seeks solutions. Confidence is the backbone of self-esteem. Without confidence, your self-esteem is shattered and you will give up before trying. Confident people are unstoppable. They may fall down, but they get up and keep trying.

Competence

"Skill comes from doing."
Ralph Waldo Emerson

Competence is more than being capable. Competence is specializing and excelling. You achieve competence by doing. Watching may make you familiar, but you will not develop skill. Competence is what separates the amateur from the professional.

The more competent you become, the more valuable you are to yourself, your family and society.

Consistency

"A half-hearted goal may get you halfway to where you want to go...but I doubt it. It's more likely to get you just as far as the first detour, and off you go in another direction."
Alec Mackenzie

Consistency is continuous effort. Consistency is necessary to achieve any goal. Inconsistency stops progress. Consistency is to life as wheels are to a bicycle. Once the wheels stop, the bicycle falls. Unless you are consistent, your efforts dilute over time making your past efforts ineffective and in vain.

Courage

"Courage is not the absence of fear, but rather the judgment that something else is more important than fear."
Ambrose Redmon

Courage is personal power. Your life grows or shrinks according to your courage. Courage sees beyond fear and sees the possibilities. A lack of courage means a life of hopelessness. When you display courage, your body, mind and spirit follow. Courage goes beyond your comfort-zone seeking new skills, experiences and opportunities.

Creativity

"The how thinker gets problems solved effectively because he wastes no time with futile "ifs" but goes right to work with the creative "how."
Norman Vincent Peale

Creative people are problem solvers. Life offers no blueprint for success or happiness. If you are not creative, you will find yourself stuck or having to pay others for solutions. Creative people live out of their imaginations. Life is a dynamic, changing place. As life evolves, solutions must also evolve. Creative people are always in demand.

Remember: *The 7 C's of Success: Character, Commitment, Confidence, Competence, Consistency, Courage and Creativity.*

The Bonus C

W hen I published the original version of this book in February 2002 under the title, *Prepare For The Wolf,* book sales immediately took off, selling thousands of copies to academia, multilevel marketing organizations, corporations, not-for-profit organizations, faith based organizations, families and individuals. Over those 10 years, I received hundreds of letters, emails and positive book reviews about the effectiveness and practicality of the concepts in the book. I have also spoken personally with readers who have thanked me for the positive impact the book has made in their life, their families, churches, schools and businesses.

Most said after reading the three mindsets- Straw, Wood and Brick, that they identified with being Wood. They agreed with my premise that they knew what they needed to do to achieve their aspirations but were not doing it. Some said they did their best to master the 7 C's of Success but being Brick was still a struggle. They had accomplished a lot more than they did prior to reading the book but were not completely satisfied even with the improvements. Something was missing.

I also have spoken to hundreds of people who said they were now Brick and experienced massive success after reading the book and applying the principles within. Some described themselves as formerly being Straw and Wood. When I asked what part of the book made the most impact and helped them achieve such success, they said it was their understanding of the books message in its entirety. They identified a common theme resonating throughout that went beyond the 7 C's of Success, overcoming the Wolves in life and comprehending the mindsets. In fact, they said the answer was revealed at the beginning of the book and referenced throughout.

To celebrate the 10th anniversary, and to better serve you on your quest to creating an extraordinary life, I have included what I am calling the Bonus C to the 7 C's of Success. It is the "C" that the Brick people I spoke with agreed was the unwritten C to the 7 C's of Success.

It is hard to hit a moving target and impossible to hit no target.

Clarity

I n order to achieve a goal, you should be specific about what you want to accomplish. You cannot go from where you are to where you want to go if you do not know exactly where you want to go. The Bonus C to the 7 C's of Success is Clarity. Clarity is defined as clearness or lucidity as to perception or understanding; freedom from indistinctness or ambiguity.

Clarity leaves no doubt about what you want to accomplish. When you are unsure, you cannot move decisively and with conviction. It is easy for the Wolf to huff and puff and blow your house in if you are not clear about your goals or if you feel lost and confused.

To achieve your aspirations and Be The Brick, you must be aware of what you want to achieve and identify the steps to make it happen. Clarity allows you to have a clear vision and an ability to articulate that vision in writing. With clarity, you are able to utilize the Law of Attraction to your advantage. The Law of Attraction is not an actual law it is a universal law that says, you attract and manifest whatever you focus on or give your energy to. This attraction happens consciously and unconsciously. With clarity, you can use the law of attraction to attract what you need to achieve your goals.

One of the most effective ways to combine clarity and the Law of Attraction to become Brick is to bring your thoughts and emotions into alignment. Meditate on your goals and feel the intensity of the emotions associated with achieving your goals. Be specific. Envision and experience the goal achieved and capture that moment in your heart, spirit and mind. See and feel it already in existence. Write this feeling down. Write down the specific goal and attach a date to when you want to accomplish it.

Do worry about how you will accomplish the goal, be flexible and allow the universe to work in your favor. How you will make it happen is not your concern in the moment. Do all you can do and believe. Feel the passion of achieving the goal and continue to work toward the goal. Feed your faith and your fears and doubts will disappear. Even when you think nothing is happening, the universe is bringing the things you need to realize your goals in alignment.

Do not give up or allow doubt to defeat you, you are closer to your aspirations than you realize. Know where you are going. Keep putting one foot in front of the other and you will arrive there. You may not achieve your exact goal but you will be a lot further along your path of success and happiness.

Remember: *Clarity is the key.*

"You have to know where you are going in

order to arrive there."

B rick people have goals, establish a plan and take action. Being Brick is challenging for most people because they do not have clear goals and they waiver in their decisions. Wavering creates confusion. You need direction and a vision. Do not be double-minded. The Bible refers to a double-minded person as being unstable. The instability is due to the confusion created in the mind about your true desires and about the right thing to do.

Make decisions based on your highest desires for your life and move in that direction. If you are going back and forth, you will soon discover you have not gotten anywhere. You are stuck, sitting on the fence and unhappy.

Just prior to releasing this book, I decided that I wanted to make some changes in my life. I wanted to maximize my opportunities. I wanted to see what is truly possible and I made some big goals. Prior to this clarity, I was unsure of what I was going to accomplish next.

The day I made the decision to make changes, I awoke early, meditated in the shower and emerged with a clear vision for my life. I knew exactly what I wanted. I even smelled the aroma from the vanilla candles burning in my new home. I captured that feeling within my heart and spirit. I saw me living this new life and wrote down what it looked and felt like. I spoke it aloud and repeated it to myself until I believed it without a doubt.

Almost magically, 14 hours later at 10:00pm, I won a brand new fully loaded Mercedes Benz. Empowered by this immediate manifestation, I began to speak everything I wanted and needed into existence. I moved with a sense of urgency towards my dream. My life moved faster in a matter of days than it did in months. I walked by faith and not by sight, never questioning the next move that I was making. I knew the vision and believed it would happen. I had no fear, no procrastination, no excuses, no doubts and no concern about anyone's support or assistance. I gave myself permission to win and went for it.

I even took two months away from business to spend exclusively with my four children who live hundreds of miles away. While with my children, I was inspired to publish a book on co-parenting, *Child Support Is More Than Money*, based on my experiences as a child of divorce and as a divorced father. In the process, I also helped my son Rob realize his dream of becoming an author and speaker where Rob is focused on helping youth and young adults realize their dreams. In the process, I accomplished my dream of having a family business established. During this time, I also assisted my beautiful and brilliant daughter, Janara, who graduated high school with honors begin her first year of college.

Determined to end the many years of copyright theft I endured with the original version of this book titled, Prepare for the Wolf, I made it my mission to develop the new and improved product you are now reading, Success Secrets from The Three Little Pigs.

All of the aforementioned occurred in a matter of months. Do not allow this moment to evade you. Use the note sections in the back of this book and clearly write down what you are passionate about and what would give your life meaning. Establish a plan of action and get started immediately. Walk by faith not by sight. Do not be detoured.

If you do not go after what you want, you will never have what you want. If you do not move forward, you will be stuck in the same place. Go for it and Be The Brick!

Remember: *Believing is seeing. Believe it and you will see it manifest in your life.*

The Steps To Developing A Brick Mindset

1. How you think is critical to your success. Be confident. Focus on success not failure. Avoid negative people and environments.

2. Clarity is key. Have clearly defined goals and dreams. Be specific and create a plan of action to achieve them.

3. Develop courage. A dream without action is nothing. Do not let anything stop you. Take custody of your life.

4. Educate yourself. Read. Acquire new skills. Be competent at what you do.

5. Be committed and consistent. Life is a voyage, set your sails for traveling the distance. Never give up!

6. Analyze details. Gather facts. Do not leave any stones unturned.

7. Plan your time and money. Do not be easily distracted. Do not settle for mediocrity or failure.

8. Be creative. Be different. Be a leader not a follower. Be you.

9. Effective communication is essential to effective leadership. Listen to and inspire the people around you.

10. Accountability. Everything starts and ends with you. If you fail to develop your character, you will discover that you are your greatest obstacle and steps 1 through 9 will not matter.

Final Thoughts

R esearch reveals that more than 80% of the world's population is not living up to their potential. It is not for a lack of information. In fact, we suffer from information overload. Unless you are living your dreams or exceeding your expectations for your life, then you are among this group of people who are not living up to their potential. You only have one life to live. Do not settle for less than you deserve.

You are born a winner. In order to live the life of a winner you must think and act like a winner. This does not mean you will not face obstacles. Even Brick faces obstacles. What it does mean is that you must learn how to effectively deal with the obstacles and challenges that life throws at you.

If you truly want to achieve success in life and business, it is not enough to apply only some of the C's. You must master and apply all of them on a regular basis. Develop the power of belief. Defeat disbelief and the negativity it creates. Visualize yourself achieving your goals and your mind will work to make it happen. Use the power of the Law of Attraction to your advantage.

Some people say, "I can" acknowledging they have the ability to achieve their goals and do not act on them. Others say, "I will" acknowledging their abilities and then defer for a later time, which usually never comes. Brick people say, "I AM." They acknowledge their abilities and do it now. They claim their goals and dreams. Brick people make things happen. Learn to make things happen!

Your mouth holds the key to your destiny. Use your words to change your world. Encourage yourself. If you use negative words, you will reap negative results. Use positive words. Count your blessings. Pray and meditate daily. Confess with your mouth the things you want and desire out of your life. Let the world know that you are confident and are committed to achieving your dreams.

Lastly, listen to your life. It will tell you what direction you are heading. If the sound of your life is growing fainter and fainter amidst the noise and constant howling of the Wolf, you are heading in the wrong direction. Turn around. You can make different choices. You are not obligated to continue following the path that you are on.

Remember: *Do not let a Wolf stop you from living your dreams.*

"Be The Brick!"

Re-Remember

Your mindset determines the quality of your choices.

Reality begins in your mind and then manifests

itself in your life.

If you fail to plan, plan to fail.

There is no next life. It is now or never.

The real pain in life is a failure to take action.

It is not enough to know what you do; you still have to do.

Brick people plan, prepare and pursue their goals.

Anyone can start; it takes a winner to finish.

You can either live your life or live your fears!

You do not have to be fearless. Just fear less.

Successful people make up their minds quickly and change them slowly.

Excuses are a curse to your goals.

Do not delay; get started today.

You paint the picture people see!

Doubt is another way of telling yourself, NO!

Do not ask why me. Instead ask, what can

I learn from this experience?

Love Yourself.

Rise above criticism and you rise above failure.

Any fool can go into debt; it takes a wise person to avoid it.

When resolving a problem,

you have to get to the root or origin of the problem.

Compete with yourself to always do better next time.

Inch by inch, it is a cinch.

A straight line is always faster than a crooked one.

Know Thyself.

You cannot move forward looking backwards,

if you do, you may stumble and fall.

Everything starts and ends with you!

The critical support you need comes from you, no one else!

Do not worry about needing help, help will find you.

Choose to Master the Seven C's and Be The Brick!

Clarity is the key.

Believing is seeing.

Believe it and you will see it manifest in your life.

Do not let a Wolf stop you from living your dreams.

"Be The Brick!"

About Robert Roots

R obert Roots is the founder of **Innerstanding™** - *Core Development Training for Organizations, Academia and Individuals.* Innerstanding™ goes beyond accountability, leadership and motivation by developing individuals from the core (inside) to make lasting positive change, increased productivity and self-efficacy based on Innerstanding™ (an awareness and appreciation for one's purpose).

An adjunct professor, life coach, consultant, author of multiple books, speaker, entrepreneur, philanthropist, founder of an award winning afterschool program, former Coral Gables, Florida and New York City Undercover Police Officer, Robert Roots was raised in one of New York City's most dangerous and impoverished housing projects with his three siblings by their divorced mother who herself was raised in a foster home.

Armed with only a high school diploma and college credits from John Jay College of Criminal Justice, Robert Roots is proof and believes, "It does not matter who you are or where you come from, you have the power to change your reality!"

Robert Roots is the author of Prepare for the Wolf (2002), now updated for its 10th Anniversary and re-titled *Success Secrets from The Three Little Pigs* (2012), and *Child Support is more than Money* (2012), written to strengthen divorced families by encouraging fathers to be involved in their children's lives and to promote co-parenting by providing effective strategies and rules of engagement.

A dedicated divorced father of four, Robert Roots is proud to have assisted his oldest son, Robert IV (Rob), release his first book and help Rob establish his speaking business focused on helping youth and young adults overcome obstacles and achieve success.

Robert Roots is available for keynotes, workshops, consulting and as a life coach.

For more information on products and services, please visit **RobertRoots.com**

Products and Other Services

For Products, Speaking, Media Interviews,

Endorsements and Consulting Services:

www.RobertRoots.com

Innerstanding™- Core Development Training for

Organizations, Academia and Individuals

www.Innerstanding.com

Contact Page

It is always a pleasure to hear from people who have read Success Secrets from The Three Little Pigs or the original version of this book, Prepare for the Wolf. If these books have benefitted you or someone you know, please share your story with me. I would love to include your testimony in my promotional materials or in my next book.

If you would like me to speak for your organization, coaching services, interested in purchasing additional copies of this book or my other products, please do not hesitate to contact me:

RR@RobertRoots.com

I look forward to hearing from you soon.

For more information, please view my websites:

www.RobertRoots.com

www.Innerstanding.com

Thank you!

Notes

Notes

Notes